JIM TURRELL

*The Gospel of*

# CAUSE

*and*

*Effect*

HEARTTALK
PUBLICATIONS

**The Gospel of Cause and Effect**
**by Jim Turrell**

HeartTalk Publications
3151 Airway Ave., K108
Costa Mesa, California 92626
714-754-7399

Copyright© 2001, 2019 by James E. Turrell
Printed in the United States of America

ISBN: 978-0-9667986-5-4

Design: slash & burn graphic design
Editor: Cynthia C. C. Cavalcanti
Proofreader: Barbara Adams

Digital Imagery: Copyright© 2001 by PhotoDisc, Inc.

# CONTENTS

# FOREWORD

In *The Science of Mind*, Ernest Homes writes, "we are likely to indulge in too much theory and too little practice" (51). By we, I gather he means metaphysicians-the thinkers and practitioners of New Thought. Sadly, Holmes' claim extends to writings in our field as well.

The book you hold in your hand represents a radical departure from abstract deliberation. What Jim Turrell offers us instead is a practically applicable model for conscious living.

Many of us read volumes, attend lectures, and participate in conferences only to find ourselves still wondering, "what does this really mean?" Often, we are too embarrassed to ask, so we take the author's/speaker's/facilitator's word for it and go on about our search. As many of you know, the word "gospel" means "good news." The good news about *The Gospel of Cause and Effect* is this: concepts that have heretofore demanded prima fade acceptance are brought to life in terms we can grasp and put to use immediately!

I speak highly of Jim's work not because I edit his writing, not because he is precious to me as a friend and a soul partner, but because he is dedicated to understanding Truth and using It in the service of happiness. May his message inspire you in deeply meaningful ways.

Cynthia C. C. Cavalcanti

# ACKNOWLEDGMENTS

With deepest appreciation, I would like to thank the people who have influenced and supported me in the writing of this book:

Ernest Holmes, founder of Religious Science and author of *The Science of Mind*, whose words never fail to inspire.

Religious Science International for giving me the opportunity to present this material as a workshop.

Cynthia Cavalcanti for editing the text, creating the layout, designing the cover, and keeping the faith.

My family and friends for encouraging my interests and supporting my work.

Finally, my colleagues, who saw value in my work and nurtured a consciousness of acceptance.

# CHAPTER 1

# INVISIBLE CAUSE

*Life flows into expression by means of an Invisible Cause. This Cause is the essence of all life and the Creative Power and Intelligence we call Spirit.*

*The nature of Cause is invisible because it is the Principle Presence of all form. Thus, it cannot be any form in particular; it can only be itself as all form.*

*This does not mean Cause is without feeling; in fact, Cause is the only real feeling of life. Cause is pure love awaiting your recognition and expression.*

# THE RULES OF CAUSE

1. Fulfillment and expansion.
2. Cooperation and harmony.
3. The ability to take form as any conceivable thing-without exception.
4. Cause is a primal substance continuously taking form.
5. Cause is void of space and time. It is only real in the here and now.
6. Cause is self-existent, self-knowing, and self-expressive.
7. Cause is forever creating a higher expression of itself.

A fundamental question to understanding the nature of existence is: Why do we exist, and what is Cause to our existence? While an academic scientist studies the nature of matter and its physical properties, the spiritual scientist studies the nature of being and the personal factors that appear to influence the life experience.

For instance, there are those who believe the nature of our being is predetermined. Others believe life is an outcome of random encounters influenced by cultural forces, identity, and fortune. Still others sense an underlying order and power that, albeit invisible to the senses, is available to the human experience through some inner connection.

Indeed, while the essence of our existence is undetectable, it is not unknowable. What seems like a contradiction is in fact an easily expressed theory that can be proven if one is able to temporarily suspend disbelief. However, before I would ask anyone to give up skepticism, I would offer the logic of my own point of view.

When I was a young boy, I received an American Flyer toy train. I recall the experience of laying out the tracks and placing the train upon them, connecting the transformer, putting the magic smoke drops into the smoke stack, plugging in, turning up the power, then watching the train start to move and miraculously pick up speed.

Once I established the correct speed to keep the train on the track, I would lay my head on the floor alongside the track. As the train passed by at eye level, barely missing my nose, it seemed as large as life. My imagination was captured. It was a heady feeling, being responsible for my imaginary passengers, making sure they were picked up and dropped off at the right places. I remember wishing I had more tracks so the journey could have lasted even longer.

The nature of Cause is much like my toy train experience. The universe has an orderly presence laid out with unimaginable complexity. And we, like the trains, seem to be placed, connected, and filled with ideas, then energized to move along cultural tracks.

We eventually learn how to control the speed of our existence, so as not to crash. Sometimes careful, sometimes reckless, we abide in our cultural circles until one day we discover a "track less traveled" (a new cultural possibility), hit the switch (change the direction of our lives), and leave the familiar, hungry for new connections.

What causes such change? I believe the human experience is complex and multifaceted.

We have an infinite supply of interests,

dreams, and possibilities, many of which are held prisoner by our cultural patterns, which obscures our connectivity and diminishes our larger sense of self. This creates an emotional vacuum, which is interpreted by our senses as emptiness.

Initially, this emptiness is seen as a symptom rather than a cause. People jump tracks and hit cultural switches because they are bored with life's foolish constancy and loath to accept responsibility for their internal discontent.

Such people will blame others for their misfortune. It is clear, however, just who has hit the switch and rewritten the script. Thus, the first rule of Cause: fulfillment and expansion.

If Cause is anything, it is the creative and essential element in every form of life-an element that is in everything, yet nothing in particular. This means the chair I am sitting in, the hand holding my pen, and the pen itself, are all Cause working in cooperation to express itself.

The second rule of Cause: cooperation and harmony. Cause has somehow harmonized the chair, hand, and pen, animating all to express the ideas in this book.

The presence of Cause initiates, animates, harmonizes, and fulfills all of what we call life, simultaneously and with no effort. Cause does all of this irrespective of religion, society, or culture. Cause is free of any and all preconceived ideas; it plays no favorites and knows nothing about anything in particular.

Confused? Think of it this way: Cause is the invisible and primal essence of everything. Even those things we may have labeled evil are filled with Cause. Even the worst inhumanity is filled with Cause.

The third rule of Cause is: the ability to take form as any conceivable thing, without exception. Before drawing the conclusion that Cause is an inherently evil concept, consider this: if Cause could judge what it creates, there would be no freedom; without the freedom for all possibilities, humanity would be no more advanced than a cow grazing in a pasture anticipating its next meal. This helps to define the fourth rule: Cause is a primal substance constantly taking-then deserting-form.

Indeed, Cause is pure, undifferentiated

substance, always available to be set into form by means of our thought or feeling. Cause must also contain said thought and feeling, thereby challenging the whole idea of its nature.

In other words, how can Cause, which is pure undifferentiated substance, also contain the very thing that would allow it to differentiate itself into some particular form? This would be the same as possessing your identity while denying you exist.

While confusing at first, the solution is simple. All form is temporary. What I have identified as me is only real in the instant I identify me.

The "me" that used to be is no longer the form Cause has taken. In fact, I can only truly be me in this instant. Hence, I am constantly taking form while simultaneously abandoning form, then taking it again.

This brings us to the fifth rule: Cause is void of space and time; it is only real in the here and now. Knowing this, you might say Cause is constantly changing into a new and infinite expression of form, fulfilling, expanding, and harmonizing itself as it goes. It is free to take any form it can conceive. Of course, this means Cause must be able to recognize itself, otherwise, how could it conceive of itself as anything?

What follows is the sixth rule: Cause is self-existent, self-knowing, and self-expressive. Cause contains an infinite idea of itself and is thus constantly changing into itself-for what else has it to change into? Lastly, the seventh and final rule: Cause is forever creating a higher expression of itself. This is only evident if you can discern progress.

Unfortunately, many are brainwashed by a media gone mad with sensational stupidity, centered on reporting that which wanders to the extreme. People will only pay for what is unbelievable.

Truth may never be profitable because Truth is not sensational. Truth is not likely to scare you or cause you to react; therefore, it is of no importance to an egocentric medium.

The subtle nature of life is never a spectacle; rather, it is a rhythmic unfoldment continually playing itself out in our experience devoid of fanfare. It is whole, filled with meaning, joy, sadness, love, emptiness, and fulfillment.

Cause-the invisible power that is forever expressing, harmonizing, and taking and abandoning form-is the constructive, self-

existent, self-knowing, and creative intelligence that brings life to all so that all may experience the blessings of being alive. Isn't it great? This is why we exist and what is Cause to our existence. But how does Cause function in the human mind? How does it translate itself into form through our mentalities?

# CHAPTER 2

# MENTALITY

*In order for Invisible Cause to manifest into Visible Effect, it must pass through your mentality. Mentality translates God's Creative Intelligence into feelings, thoughts, desires and initiative. Your mentality is a direct link to Spirit.*

*All aspects of your life, without exception, pass from Cause through your mentality into effect. There is no other passage.*

*There is only one Mind, God's Mind, but there are many different mentalities.*

# THE RULES OF MENTALITY

1. Life is not out of order, just spinning.
2. What you think about all day long, you become.
3. Always follow your heart.

The nature of Cause, while invisible, does have a translating mechanism-mentality. Before I explore the structure of mentality, I must emphasize all the ideas I am proposing may not be true.

The ideas I am suggesting are based on a spiritual way of thinking and perceiving intended to improve and expand your life experience. Reading this book will inform and, more importantly, may open some mental doors and help you see the sacred value of your existence.

I believe we are all sacred, even those of whom we may not approve. Once you change your mind about life, this particular way of thinking can seem like a miracle. You become what I call "a useful person," able to make meaningful contributions. To become such a useful person, you must become familiar with who you are intellectually and what you are as the medium of Cause.

A medium is a means of creative expression. In art, the medium might be oil paints, marble, or clay; in music, a violin, piano, or flute. In the basics of Cause and Effect, the medium through which Cause finds passage into the human experience is mentality.

Each of us has a mentality we use to translate Cause into ideas, feelings, thoughts, desires, and initiative. Entailed in our mentality is everything we have ever seen, felt, reacted to, learned, known, and experienced.

In addition, our mentality is connected to a vast reservoir of all humanity's memory. This collective memory is called our "race mind."

The influence of race mind is immense and largely subconscious. It is intellectually indictable while still operating in our decision-making processes. Later, in Chapter Four, I will examine the influence of race mind and how to detect its presence.

Mentality also has a direct connection to Cause. Cause, however, speaks through a component of mentality known as intuition. Intuition is different from intellect because it is not limited to what it has learned, experienced, or habitualized. Intuition is the immediate experience and expansion of knowledge providing information over, above, and beyond the sense-bound secular knowledge of the intellect.

Intellect is important, but not more so than intuition. The intellect is not a thinker; it is a calculator that weighs, measures, compares, analyzes, predicts, and labels. More about the intellect is covered in Chapter Six.

It is important to emphasize intuition because it is your most valuable ally. In mentality, intuition is directly linked to your intuitive sense of existence.

It is this internal knowing, unbound by conventional humanity, that is the creative genius in your mentality. There are many mentalities with many intellectual and cultural identities, but there is only one Cause that can expand and harmonize the human race, and that is intuition.

Intuition is central to your revelation of Cause. It is the one component of your mentality that can expose your sacred connectivity. It heals and unifies because it is the only part of us that can neutralize the pain and insanity of judgment.

The negative judgments of the race mind have been memorized to a point that we have intellectually accepted our prejudice as a viable mode of thought and behavior. Prejudice disconnects your mind from your heart, creating political head-trips that spin your life into oblivion-and spinning can make you dizzy.

The first rule of mentality: life is not out of order, just spinning. To put your life back in order, you must stop spinning long enough to see who you are in relationship to Cause. This requires familiarity with your spirituality, your psychology, and your philosophical perception.

Your mentality has two components that determine your impressions, experiences, and behavior: intellect and intuition. Both are required for a meaningful existence.

While I examine these as separate entities, they are but two sides of one coin: Cause. Intuition without intellect results in an unfulfilled dream; intellect without intuition is an exercise in futility.

Mentality is also the container of two spiritual components commonly called Soul and Spirit.

Soul is the sacred realm of your intuition and Spirit is the sacred realm of your intellect.

It is important to note that while there is not "your" soul and spirit or "my" soul and spirit, there is that portion of Soul and Spirit we call our own. There is only one Soul or Spirit, and we can increase our portion of it if we understand our infinite power and intellectual ability to choose a way of living that is meaningful and giving.

The difficulty in having so many names for the components of mentality is the confusion it creates around the nature of who we are. This confusion surrounds the issue of spirituality and is often misinterpreted as not spiritual, but psychological or mental.

Sometimes confusion is necessary for growth; it is an indication we are expanding, growing, and becoming more of who we are as Spirit. Think of it as an opportunity to deconstruct the order of those thoughts and things that are no longer useful.

Do you believe in a power greater than you are? Is that power detached from you or part of you? For those who have a predetermined ideal of a divine power that is separate and detached from their existence, this book will be a different view. For those who see Spirit as inescapably connected to their own individual existence, this book might help form the basis for a deeper ideal and a richer experience.

While mentality may seem removed from your spiritual sense of self, it is still your portion of Spirit functioning at the level of your concept of it. This, in part, explains the second rule of mentality: what you think about all day long, you become.

Mentality is a rudder. It does not power your life, but it does provide signals that help guide its eternal existence. The only mistake is to believe you are the power, the guidance, and the experience.

Unfortunately, mentality is a word that poorly

describes the translator's role. Again, while knowing about your mentality is central to understanding your relationship to Cause, do not become overly impressed by or reliant upon its linear role in this model. Rather, use your understanding to deepen your relationship beyond words. Then train your intellect to spot the presence of your spirit and soul in all you say, do, and express. Hence, the third rule of mentality: always follow your heart.

# CHAPTER 3

# VISIBLE EFFECT

*All life, from feeling to form and reaction to action, is an effect. If you can feel it or sense it, it is an effect.*

*All effects are temporary. They do not last, but they can be repeated. The important thing to remember about effects is the only meaning they have is what we give them.*

*Do not give meaning to an effect that would hurt, harm, or take away life from you or another.*

# THE RULES OF EFFECT

1. All effects are temporary. The only meaning they have is what we give them.
2. Society evolves as it informs itself and changes its collective mind.
3. Every effect we can see or feel owes its existence to Cause.
4. All effects are subject to change and were never intended for or capable of an infinite existence.

The most powerful human encounter is the external, phenomenal world of effect. Effect is the empirical, sense-bound visible world that stimulates our visceral perception. It is what seems to create the conditions and circumstances we experience with varying degrees of positive and negative results.

The world of effect appears real, solid, and permanent, but is actually a temporary and soluble reaction to what we believe. The first rule of effect: all effects are temporary and the only meaning they have is what we give them. Do not assign meaning to a person, place, condition, or circumstance that would hurt, harm, or marginalize.

This may be hard to do because many of us are predisposed to habitual patterns that usurp all conscious thought. The primary cause of this "displacement" is race mind: humanity's cauldron of emotional memory that compels our behavior every time the external world of effect stimulates a response. This stimulus response experience fools us into believing effect is Cause.

For instance, if someone is rude, many people have a built-in "rude response" ready to take unconscious control when stimulated. This makes the rude person appear to be the source of our response.

This stimulus response is observable in some authority figures, because authority figures are mostly governed by rules, not consciousness. In most cases, irrespective of motive, behavior is the decisive factor of character and value.

A person whose character slips is not only

judged, but also devalued and alienated. This is a natural consequence in most social groupings. However, the stigma that is held in race memory stays attached to the individual and anybody who looks or acts like that individual, until a conscious awakening informs the culture or society that the prejudice held is no longer necessary.

The second rule: society evolves as it informs itself and changes its collective mind. Part of the purpose of this book is to support and assist in this change of mind and heart.

What happens in the world has only one Cause and that Cause is invisible. For instance, one might say the reason he or she plays golf is to enjoy the game, the beauty of the golf course, or the fun of making a good shot.

Cause, however, is more than a reason for someone's behavior. It is the remarkable order that holds all the atoms and molecules in place as the ball, the course, the club, and the player. Third rule: every effect we can see or feel owes its existence to Cause.

This knowledge determines where we must center our attention if we want to change or expand our life experience. This brings us back to the first rule of effect: the only meaning anything has is what we give it. Do not underestimate the importance of this rule. It is pivotal in all your decision-making processes. Effects, felt or seen, are temporary. The fourth rule: all effects are subject to change and were never intended for or capable of an infinite existence. Those who seek meaning in the world of effect are destined to become confused and fearful because they concoct and attach a meaning that only exists in their mind.

Whatever happens *to* you happens *through* you. Your condition or circumstance is not solid or real. It only appears real because the intellect and ego are not informed enough to fathom a larger Cause. Most have overdeveloped their reliance on sense-bound perception and, hence, remain the prisoners of limited knowledge and superstition.

This is most apparent in religion and politics— two dominant sources that affect how we view, behave in, and react to the world. If you want to teach unity, you must be informed by something other than circumstance or condition.

Effect is a powerful drug-like experience that can put you to sleep, awakening you only when a knee-jerk reaction is required. To fully awaken, it helps to know the internal nature of mentality: how it works, what it responds to, and how to use it.

To understand mentality, the bridge between cause and effect, it helps to see it as a bipartite construct consisting of Spirit, the objective director, and Soul, the subjective servant. This director-servant relationship is central to gaining creative dominion in the decision-making process for which we are all responsible.

# CHAPTER 4

# SOUL

*The subjective Soul is the servant and creative power of your mentality. It contains your intuition, the sacred potential inherent in all life.*

*Your intuition is filled with creative ideas and feelings and is a tremendous power for good that must be consciously directed. It also contains your memory, the storehouse of cultural patterns held as emotional reactions destined to repeat in the absence of conscious direction.*

| SUBJECTIVE SOUL<br>CREATIVE (subconscious) | |
| --- | --- |
| **INTUITION** | **MEMORY** |
| Universal Subjective Potential<br>The creative ideal and feeling of<br>Universal Intelligence.<br>CREATES ITSELF NEW<br>WHEN CONSCIOUSLY<br>DIRECTED | Collective Human Memory<br>The reactive and emotional<br>patterns of thought.<br>REPEATS ITSELF OLD<br>IN THE ABSENCE<br>OF DIRECTION |

Many people seek control of their lives, desperately trying to feel stable in the face of uncertainties. Their efforts are mighty but doomed to failure because their attention is focused on effect: an illusion of permanence too tempting to resist.

Effect is the same illusion that led the Greeks to assume the Earth was the unstable and uncertain home of humanity, while the sky and the heavens were the peaceful and permanent home of the gods. For thousands of years, humanity labored under this misinformed premise, primarily because of sense-bound empirical observations that could never detect exploding stars, black holes, or galaxies in various stages of taking and deserting form. Misinformed or not, however, something within humanity is permanent, stable, and completely reliable—the Soul.

The nature of the Soul is always in dominion but never in control. It is the worker, the creative intelligence that simultaneously creates, sustains, and expresses form. It is the actor and the repository of memory, not the director or decision maker. That is Spirit, and I will discuss the nature of Spirit in the next chapter.

As creator, your soul is connected to Cause through your intuitive mentality: a universal potential filled with creative possibilities awaiting our demand. The problem is, very few are willing to make the demand because few are aware they have the right.

Most of humanity ignores their intuition because they do not believe they have the capability or the right to demand an original life. It is our foolish consistencies that absent our awareness disconnecting us from what matters in favor of what needs our attention.

What drags us away from the very thing that can revive us? Memory, a component of our soul that holds the sum total of all our emotional and reactive patterns, and the collective emotional memory of the entire human race. If left undirected, the soul's memory must keep repeating our emotional patterns, recreating our experiences until we awaken and reclaim dominion of our existence.

The subjective Soul is a powerful ally when consciously directed. Once you put a demand, filled with conviction and feeling, upon your soul, it is compelled to create and repeat the pattern until you demand a different result.

The important part of the Soul's job is to never question the demand. Moment to moment, and millennium to millennium, the Soul faithfully recreates humanity's collective fears, doubts, and insanity.

Gradually, however, humanity is awakening to its power, and more and more people are demanding a spiritual existence with a greater experience of love. This demand is changing the race mind of humanity, reconnecting life to the magnificent potential of Cause.

One way to detect the presence and operation of the soul is to live in a 48-hour window: never more than 24 hours behind or ahead of yourself in your reactions to life's experience. This requires discipline because it asks you to set aside your history and speculative nature, instructing your intellect to cease all review of the past or speculation of the future.

This is similar to freeing up disk space on a computer. It gives you the opportunity to recognize the reality of the moment. Living in the "here and now" helps to remove the unrelenting pressure of the "then and later." It also assists in detecting our intuition and the presence of our portion of soul.

Combine your presence of mind with your presence of soul, and the very nature of life reveals its genius. Not only will you be informed, you will be inspired. Such inspiration does more than solve problems; it provides an understanding that initiates new responses, new direction, and new life.

An important rule for staying in the 48-hour window is to never exaggerate or minimize what you are experiencing. Instead, learn to report your experience to yourself as if reporting the events, conditions, circumstances, people, feelings, and reactions to a neutral third party.

This is not a reality check. "Reality check" is a popular term that claims to be reporting the facts of something as if they were "the truth," i.e., fixed, inescapable, and absolute. This is neither truth nor reality; it is the reporting of your impressions of a direct experience reflecting what you know about reality. Reality is infinite and impossible to report, but not impossible to know.

Again, I emphasize there is only infinite reality, unbound by precedent, and each of us has our portion. Said portion reflects how we are informed about what we know of ourselves. If you define soul as something separate from Cause—a distant power disconnected from its creation—you must abandon faith in favor of hope and fate. In that scenario, hope is an empty promise of better days in a distant life far removed from the burdens of doubt and despair, and fate is a run of good luck.

Faith, on the other hand, offers no answers, separation, fortune, or hope. Faith is the inexorable knowing that you are connected to an ineffable, sacred Cause that cannot know you as something different from itself. Once you prove the link, you release the only real power of life:

the love of Cause.

When the Cause of love is recognized as the love of Cause, then love is released like a flow of sacred reality animating every form of life. It is the soul's desire expressing a greater life so that all may know the freedom of love.

of cause. Men through blindness have followed
and called actions a part of nature, but before
this, actions are expressions of spirit, which alone
may show the freedom of man.

# CHAPTER 5

# SPIRIT

*The objective Spirit can select and initiate, but it cannot create. It is the seat of your intuitive nature, your connection to intuition giving you unlimited access to all knowledge, but it requires a willing and receptive faith in order to reveal its treasure.*

*It also contains your intellectual ability, the power to choose a state of mind that is either willing or willful, receptive or demanding. It is limited by what it has learned and experienced.*

| OBJECTIVE SPIRIT | |
|---|---|
| SELECTIVE (conscious) | |
| INTUITIVE | INTELLECTUAL |
| Willing and Receptive Operates out of belief, acceptance, and faith. UNLIMITED ACCESS TO THE KNOWLEDGE OF ALL LIFE | Willful and Demanding Can operate out of fear, rejection, and disbelief. LIMITED BY WHAT IT HAS LEARNED AND EXPERIENCED |

Every creation is preceded by an ideal—some initiating thought that becomes the embryonic catalyst and compels the Soul to take form. Much like soil compels the seed to grow, creating the experience of the plant, your thoughts compel your portion of soul to create an experience of your ideal. But what created the seed? What created the thought?

Perhaps the most loaded word in self-help vocabulary is ego. Ego, not accurately known, is popularly defined as the self-centered part of each person that presumes they are the hub of the universe, the creator of life.

When in control, the ego cancels the existence of Cause as an infinite presence in which we exist, in favor of itself as the only presence of life existing in the world of effect, a world the ego must conquer, control, and direct, if it is to survive. The law of ego is: control your environment and conquer all who threaten your way of life. This way of egocentric living is oddly focused more on the possibility of death than the probability of life.

One way to free yourself from this mindset is to move your perception of reality into a 48- hour window and free yourself from the tyranny of history. Such is the power of your spirit. Spirit is the directive presence of consciousness: the awareness of who you are based in the here and now experience of your life.

Ralph Waldo Emerson saw life as biography rather than as history. History objectifies the past as a harbinger of the future; biography subjectifies the present as a moveable feast.

Your portion of Spirit is a reflection of consciousness. If your consciousness is limited by the contracted belief in your past, then little of what is called your original self can be detected. But if you stay in the 48-hour window, your original self will emerge providing new ideas, thoughts, and knowledge.

Some mistakenly seek this window by

numbing their consciousness with alcohol and/ or drugs. This does not work because the self must be fully awake in order to receive the experience of life. Numbness is escape from reality. If you are willing to encounter reality in the window, fully awake, you will inevitably detect your spirit and claim your right and responsibility to select and initiate your existence.

Spirit, like Soul, is infinite and unitary. There is not your spirit or my spirit, there is just Spirit, and our portion of Spirit is central to our experience of life.

The more Spirit you decide to embody, the more life is available for you to experience. In this way, Spirit is like land. The more you possess, the more you can grow. The more you grow, the more you can share. Spirit can also be thought of as a container. The larger the container, the more of life you can partake of and know. The more you know of life, the more generous you can be in living.

Spirit, however, must be seen in this model as that portion of consciousness available to receive the original and new ideas, thoughts, and concepts that will help us distinguish and define our presence in the world. The smaller our consciousness, the lesser the flow; the larger our consciousness, the more that can become ours to live.

Spirit is thus synonymous with knowing, but not creating. Spirit is the thinker; Soul is the actor. Belief is the bridge that links both to the infinite cause and effect of who we really are.

Spirit is the part of me I must expand if I am to have a richer experience of life. If I believe the nature of Spirit is the director of life, I can release my egocentric behavior, which wastes my time trying to control my existence, in favor of Spirit-centered behavior, which fills my life with the ultimate activity of belief—the contemplation of spiritual power.

When Spirit is in charge, I experience the peaceful presence of Cause. When ego is in charge, I experience the conflicted hope of my future alongside the conflicted fear of my past. Is there a choice? Always! Do I detect the choice? Not always!

How do we miss the presence of Spirit? We are

not trained or educated to see it as something in which we exist. Instead, most of the Western world is trained to survive and educated to hope. We are not trained to live creatively or spiritually.

Much of our knowledge of Spirit is relegated to religions that are in large part driven by fear and superstition, or a psychology of life controlled by a mechanistic sort of hope that marginalizes the genius of our original self.

Spirit, however, is destined to overcome all obstacles. Spirit is forever providing an infinite supply of new and creative thoughts. As you awaken to Spirit's existence, your life gradually expands, sequentially offering you a greater here and now, and cumulatively acquiring more consciousness, a greater portion of Spirit.

Your portion of Spirit reflects your intuitive powers. Spirit is your intuitive nature linking your intuition to Soul and opening the door to Cause. Once you realize the existence of your intuitive link to Cause, your depth of knowledge will reveal a life previously unknown to you.

This is not a psychic reading; it is a mystical experience that shows you the reality of your presence, not the facts or personality of your existence. The difference is important because many mistakenly seek spiritual truth in a psychic reading of personality. Personality is not reality; rather, it is the sum total of what you have learned or experienced.

Such information is obviously limited because it can only show you the surface of where you have been and the direction you seem to be pointed. Spirit is not concerned with your past, future, direction, or origin.

Spirit is only available in the here and now and is unlimited in what it can reveal as to the depth of your existence. Such revelation creates a new landscape free from judgment, fear, and doubt—a landscape where you are free to move in any direction.

Spirit is original. Memory is repetitive. Memory can function as an ally when you give it a steady diet of new and creative thoughts that come from your original sense of self.

Spirit fills your memory with creative feelings and thoughts. This stimulates the intellect to start weighing, measuring, labeling, and analyzing while the soul animates Spirit's creative flow into new feelings and experiences.

As long as you are receptive, Spirit's intuitive nature will use the Soul's connection to Cause, opening up an avenue for new and original thinking that is often described as an "ah-ha," but decidedly more intense. Many people are surprised by this feeling and deem it unusual or abnormal. This is unfortunate because it frequently keeps people from developing the consciousness that could, indeed, make the experience a normal occurrence.

To create a spiritual lifestyle, let us now examine the tools and powers that make this possible: tools of the intellect and powers of the intuition.

# CHAPTER 6

# TOOLS OF THE INTELLECT

*The intellect is basically a calculator that cannot be turned off Its tools continue to operate upon whatever you think, feel, or desire.*

*If you are fearful, its tools will center your attention on fear and continue to manifest and justify your experience of lack and limitation. Instead, use your intellectual tools to center your thoughts, feelings, and desires upon. the unlimited good of your intuitive powers, e.g., a greater life, love, joy, peace, etc.*

# TOOLS OF THE INTELLECT

PREDICT

CONTROL

ANALYZE

WEIGH

MEASURE

COMPARE

LABEL

Many link intellectual capacity to the ability to think, i.e., the more my intellect contains, the greater my ability to think. The drawback to this assumption is that the intellect is not the thinker.

The intellect can contain, construct, plan, analyze, and, like a gardener, trim and cut our growth, but it cannot think. Thinking is the function of intuition, and Cause, linked to our mentality through our intuition, is the only provider of new and original ideas. Cause is the thinker.

The intellect functions much like a tool used in building a house. It cuts thoughts and ideas into pieces, then measures and connects those pieces, giving shape and structure to the way we live. It can also deconstruct, remodel, and repeat itself, but it cannot create a new thought structure.

The power to create is strictly intuitive. The intellect's tools include the ability to weigh, measure, compare, analyze, predict, and control. The need to control and predict is epidemic in the world and frequently leads to the very result it is used to avoid helplessness!

The ability to control oneself and predict outcomes is a sought-after quality. People succeed and fail, their relationships rise and fall, and their businesses function and malfunction because so many are accustomed to predicting outcomes and controlling their lives.

The misuse of these abilities is not, however, an inherent flaw. It is a misunderstanding of the form, function, and automatic nature of life to create itself into a greater and more complex experience.

The tools of the intellect, powered by the

qualities of our intuition, can create a consciousness of ease, functionality, and constructive form. But intellect, absent these powers, loses its potency. When sterile and lacking conviction, the intellect can behave like a disease, infecting life with the collective doubt, fear, and guilt so well-rehearsed by humanity.

In this condition, the intellect seeks to solve its problematic self by recreating the same circumstance and predicting a new outcome. This is the classic definition of insanity: thinking, acting, and behaving the same way while expecting a different result. No amount of analysis of this condition will change it. No amount of control will keep it from giving you the same result.

The intellect does not need to be changed or controlled, but our perception of its function does. The intellect is an important part of our mentality. It gives us the tools but cannot provide the power or originality of Cause. Power is the function of our intuition.

# CHAPTER 7

# POWERS OF THE INTUITION

*The powers of your intuition are creative and intelligent and await your recognition and utilization. They are the perfect companion powers created to work in total cooperation with your intellectual tools. They complete your mentality by becoming "Power Tools" you can use to create a sacred eternity.*

*Why not predict a life of light, peace, beauty, truth, joy, and love? Why not control your experience of acceptance with unconditional love?*

# POWERS OF THE INTUITION

LIFE

LOVE

BEAUTY

TRUTH

JOY

PEACE

POWER

When someone is asked to define the word "power" relative to the human experience, a frequent response is, "an authority that controls behavior based on consequence or punishment." For instance, a robber may use the threat of violence to control a circumstance influencing the behavior of a victim to hand over the money or risk being killed.

This type of scenario is played out continually in relationships, prisons, businesses, politics, religion, education, and medicine, to name a few.

But power can be defined and experienced as something other than behavior controlled by consequences. Power, in sacred terms, can be understood as life predicting love, controlling behavior with peace, or beauty influencing the immediate experience of truth through a reality of joy.

For example, it is possible that a spiritually informed person could, in the face of intimidation, respond with love instead of fear. Such a response would do more than change the outcome; it would transform the very nature of the intimidator and the one responding with love.

How do we become spiritually informed? By paying attention to what our intuition is telling us about our functionality in the world.

A grain of sand functions as part of a beach. Its purpose is defined, in part, by the role it plays in giving the beach its functional nature. This does not give meaning to the beach. It merely reveals the function of one of its parts, helping us see the law of cooperation and harmony in action. Meaning is what we attach to the beach in response to what we feel and know.

In a similar fashion, individual human beings are made up of a complex combination of structures cooperating in harmony to define, in part, the role we play in giving life its functional nature. The meaning of that nature, however, is what we attach to life based, in some measure, on what we know, how we have been conditioned to respond, and what we feel we need. In addition, our functional nature, empowered with varying degrees of fear and or love, assigns meaning to life, the beach, and anything else with which we interact.

Powered with love, the function of life can constructively utilize its intellectual tools to create new and original definitions and meanings that reveal the effortless laws of complexity at work. This expands our protean ability (our ability to shape our thoughts to fit our values) to become more of what we desire to experience by harmonizing the multitudinous incongruities. This represents our ability to shift the shape of our thoughts, which gives us the consciousness to grow and move simultaneously in many different directions.

For example, if your desire is to learn how to

sail, your intellect will conspire to gather all that is needed to learn how to sail. As you learn, you become a sailor, harmonizing your fears and your ignorance with your desires, creating an ability to effortlessly integrate sailing into all your other activities.

This is the power of intuition: an authority that creates the consciousness or mindset of the experience and, at the same time, fulfills, expands, and harmonizes every human contradiction. Powered by fear, the function of life is forced to construct defensive and offensive mechanisms to control and protect its station, status, and property. This multiplies our incongruities and creates a consciousness that restricts our movement and channels our fear into survival.

The intuition is the seat of the Soul's power. Beauty, peace, joy, love, light, and truth are the· real intuitive powers of life. Money, authority, status, possessions, and weapons are props used to create the illusion of power; they are pieces of a misinformed life constantly lost, then· gained, then lost again in an epic battle for control. These pieces have no meaning and offer only despair, fear, and false hope.

The powers of intuition, on the other hand, offer a reality that does not need to be controlled, only exercised. What if you could see the beauty that surrounds you? What if life were a constant stream of light animating your eternal truth, giving you the freedom to live and create a greater experience? Would it not be worth your while to learn how to live such a life? Your choice: expectancy or expectation.

# CHAPTER 8

# EXPECTATION

*Expectation comes from the memorized episodes of humanity's fears, failures, and rejections, experienced and emotionally stored/ stuffed into our subjective memory—a race mind to which we are all connected. Unfortunately, in our efforts to prevent experiences of failure and fear, expectations can become the center of our attention and recreate themselves simply because Cause only hears the affirmative, i.e., Cause does not hear the **don't** in, "I don't want the pain."*

*Expectations are subtle-pay attention!*

# RESULTS OF EXPECTATION

FAILURE

REJECTION

DISAPPOINTMENT

UNHAPPINESS

LONELINESS

POVERTY

DISEASE

*What you think about all day long, you become.*

Initially, the difference between expectation and expectancy escapes most people because both words seem to mean the same thing. The distinction between the two, however, is crucial to developing a spiritual philosophy.

We all have expectations. We all expect life to behave and respond in a certain way. If life fails to give us what we want, our expectations become "unmet expectations."

If we have enough unmet expectations, our intellect becomes conditioned to search our memory for solutions and answers to such empty questions as: What went wrong? How do I correct my mistake? What do I have to do to improve so this type of experience will not recur?

Expectations, no matter how we look at them, force life into a timeframe of past, present, and future scenarios that require solutions. This causes life to be perceived as a dysfunctional and mistake-laden experience requiring correction, improvement, and analysis to a never-ending flow of problems.

How can you think of love or peace when there are so many "unmet expectations?" Thoughts of peace, love, life, joy, and light seem absurd when life is filled with so many unresolved crises.

Most people are simply too overwhelmed by expectations to employ the powers of spirit or intuition. Most are conditioned to turn to the power of the intellect and try to think their way out of the box or hope some distant spiritual power will magically lift them out of their circumstances.

This is the way the ego or intellect traps people

into degrees of satisfaction or dissatisfaction, failure or success, and rejection or acceptance, turning attention and behavior to managing, resolving, or avoiding the conflict rather than healing it once and for all. Thus, life's unresolved issues remain the focus and force of our lives, requiring all of our time, energy, and resources to fix the problems.

If you line up the tools of your intellect on one side, the powers of your intuition on the other, and place your expectations in the middle, your time, energy, and resources are going to be totally dedicated to correcting the problems of failure, rejection, disappointment, unhappiness, loneliness, poverty, or disease. The powers of your intuition will become attached to your expectations, creating an endless loop of problems.

| POWERS OF THE INTUITION | EXPECTATION | TOOLS OF THE INTELLECT |
|---|---|---|
| Life | Failure | Predict |
| Love | Rejection | Control |
| Beauty | Disappointment | Analyze |
| Peace | Unhappiness | Weigh |
| Joy | Loneliness | Measure |
| Truth | Poverty | Compare |
| Light | Disease | Label |
| (understanding) | | |

Examine the consequences of expectations. If they become the focus of your thought process, they result in the following types of beliefs:

- A life of failure becomes predictable.
- Your experience of love is controlled by fear of rejection.
- The beauty of existence is lost in the analysis of your disappointments.
- The weight of your unhappiness is magnified by your lack of peace.
- Loneliness is measured by your joyless relationships.
- Poverty becomes your truth in a comparison of those who have more than you.
- Disease is a label frequently attached to your sense of health.

To further understand what it means to live in expectation, examine the following scenario:

# HISTORY IS MY EXPERIENCE

*(Read aloud. How much of this is true?)*

*My relationships carry a heavy sense of EXPECTATION. They depend on my ability to know my past and repeat what used to work, correct what went wrong, or imitate what works for others.*

*My sense of history keeps teaching me how to justify myself, improve myself, and envy those who seem to know more than I know. My sense of the future is based on how well I speculate, guess, or hope.*

*Most of my relationships work, but no matter how hard I try to be satisfied, I know there will be disappointments. No matter how much success I have, I know there is always some failure.*

*Regardless of acceptance, I still experience rejection. No matter what, intimacy is still a problem I must solve. This is my attitude:*

*Because I am convinced by my history of what happened to me, I must look carefully at my present conditions and future possibilities. The choices I make for my future will be based on what I need to avoid, must learn how to handle, or I know I must solve before I can be happy. Intimacy is mostly problematic for me, but I know that one day I will find the right relationship that will meet all my expectations.*

Living in your history shows you what you have been thinking and how you tend to react, but it cannot teach you anything you do not already know. The activity of education is not what is behind you; it is the pathway before you. When you step forward into the unknown, what you learn is measured by the size of your step and your intention as you take it.

Cause cannot dictate what we think. Expectations, even those of success and happiness, are always accompanied by their opposites. You cannot have one without the other, and no matter how sincerely you want more acceptance and less rejection, or more wealth without poverty, your focus will always be on the problem of what you do not want. Expectations will always lead to a problematic lifestyle. Only a life of expectancy can give what you truly want.

# CHAPTER 9

# EXPECTANCY

*Expectancy is the action of the here and now. Expectancy is a consciously consistent attitude that knows only good will prevail, no matter what happens.*

*Expectancy is an affirmative awareness of success, acceptance, satisfaction, happiness, prosperity, health, and loving relationships. It attaches no meaning to the past and gives nothing to the future except its loving presence.*

*Expectancy draws the greatest good from Invisible Cause and is only available in the moment.*

# RESULTS OF EXPECTANCY

SUCCESS

ACCEPTANCE

SATISFACTION

HAPPINESS

RELATIONSHIPS

PROSPERITY

HEALTH

*What you think about all day long, you become.*

As explained in the previous chapter, expectations are part of a silent thought process that can narrow your thinking and keep your life problematical. Expectancy, on the other hand, is the focus of a conscious thought process that expands your awareness and keeps you aware of the dynamic nature of life and the powerful presence of Cause working as the agent of change.

Expectancy can do this because it centers your attention on the perfect outcome, not the worst-case scenario. This sounds crazy, of course, to the egocentric "past-driven" person whose primary responsibility is to cite and assign blame, guilt, and fear as the causes for failure, rejection, or loss.

Expectancy frees the mind from looking for what or who is responsible for the condition of life by examining the power that creates a new experience. Expectancy opens the door to the power of Cause—a dynamic idea that informs the intellect as to what is really important, such as· love, beauty, peace, joy, truth, life, and light (light means understanding).

Once informed, the intellect can let go of its willful ways and begin to work in cooperation with Cause. This opens the means for an expanded way of perception and thought by consciously directing your thought to a higher ideal. This action invites your intuition to enlighten your creative ability, guiding your thinking away from the old blame game toward new ideas that promote productive outcomes and behavior.

Expectancy connects you to the power of

Cause through the Principles representative of that power: Love, Light, Joy, Peace, Beauty, Life, and Truth. Once connected, you can release the past and embrace the moment. You can literally feel your intuition begin to school you on behavior, vocabulary, concept, and perception. In an instant, your entire sense of life can expand into a panorama of comprehension giving you access to knowledge you could never have achieved through your intellect.

As such, expectancy is the greatest secret revealed about healing one's own mind and feelings. It is an oasis in the desert of despair, a breath of fresh air taken from the highest possible thought you can think.

Expectancy centers the energy of attention individualizing the power of a positive and productive thought. Your feelings are directed into the most dynamic action possible. Energy, form, and power become the bywords of the expectancy-focused mind.

When you line up your powers of intuition with a consciousness of expectancy, your intellect becomes a powerful tool for transformation.

Words, actions, and creative ideas spring from a well of optimism. Success, acceptance, satisfaction, happiness, relationships, prosperity, and health literally invoke the power of Cause to manifest your life.

| POWERS OF THE INTUITION | EXPECTANCY | TOOLS OF THE INTELLECT |
|---|---|---|
| Life | Success | Predict |
| Love | Acceptance | Control |
| Beauty | Satisfaction | Analyze |
| Peace | Happiness | Weigh |
| Joy | Relationships | Measure |
| Truth | Prosperity | Compare |
| Light | Health | Label |
| (understanding) | | |

Examine the consequences of expectancy. A life of success becomes predictable. Your experience of love is controlled by your acceptance of life.

The beauty of your existence is found in the analysis of your blessings. Your peace of mind magnifies your happiness by outweighing all apparent discord and doubt.

Joy is not measured by the success of your relationships; rather, it is a power you bring to your relationships that allows you to measure your growth and expansion. Prosperity is no longer determined by comparisons with others; instead, it is the outcome of a Principle of Truth in which comparisons are about how you hold yourself as the sacred creation of Cause versus the secular product of effect. Health is a matter of using the power of light (spiritual understanding) to melt the darkness and morbidity of the world of effect, giving you the power to label your presence as whole and complete, even in the face of labels that would have you depressed and worried.

To better understand the difference between living in expectation and expectancy, examine the following scenario:

## MY LIFE IS A DYNAMIC BIOGRAPHY

*(Read aloud. How much of this is true?)*

*Life is a great adventure because I know it is always revealing a greater good. My attitude is one of expectancy (knowing all works for my good) because I live in the here and now.*

*My three greatest attributes are intensity, energy, and power. Every idea I have adds to my creative life a sense of attraction.*

*I am focused on creating a "me" that is irresistible to its perfect right relationship. My energy moves me in an orderly fashion, demonstrating a form and order that is uniquely mine.*

*The power I feel comes from being so clear on what I want that I model for others the joy of being direct, honest, and supportive. No matter what I do, I continuously feel a growing sense of confidence, cooperation, and productivity.*

*Every relationship we have is a blessing. This is my attitude:*

*I see the spiritual purpose of my life. I am convinced of my divine dynamic presence and its individualized uniqueness. I celebrate the intensity, energy and power that is mine to apply.*

*In every relationship I have I am specific, clear, definite, and willing to accept the outcome as my good demonstrated at the level of my thought. The changes of my life are based on my ability to think, speak and act in a productive, constructive, and affirmative manner.*

As you can see, a life perceived as a dynamic biography is not concerned with judgments of how things used to be or could be. Instead, a life of dynamic biography is a life of expectancy, lived in the here and now, filled with as much good as anyone can conceive. The result of such good is beyond our comprehension until we think with the logic of the *Gospel of Cause and Effect.*

The purpose of exploring this topic is to invite you into a new world that is awake and alive. Why would you want to live in a world that is numb and unconscious?

As you read the concluding chapter, work with the idea that there is a reality already in existence, waiting for you to expand your mentality, spread your intuitive wings, and fly high into a greater and more creative life.

# CHAPTER 10

# CONCLUSION

*Rethink your existence and draw a new result from the infinite presence of Cause. If you want a greater life, change your mind and keep it changed.*

# INVISIBLE CAUSE

Every result or outcome is caused by something. This is easy to see in the physical world.

For instance, a baseball is thrown because a player is playing a game that requires that action. In a very simple sense, the game is the cause and the outcome is the action.

The player, however, is motivated by a mental cause that is driven, in part, by the need or desire for success, status, or love of the game. Mental cause, while invisible to the eye, is experienced through the feelings and reactions of the player, as in the thrill of victory or the agony of defeat.

What cause gives rise to physical and mental cause? What holds the ball, the player, and the baseball park together?

That Cause is invisible and is the progenitor of existence itself. It holds together our lives, our world, and the entire universe.

Everything, without exception, flows from this Invisible Cause, including the physical and mental causes of our experiences. This means the

Invisible Cause to all life is self-existent, self-knowing, and self-expressive. It is cause to its own experience. We may call this Cause Spirit, God, Supreme Being, or something like this.

## MENTALITY

Because every form of existence was first an idea or feeling, it had to manifest through something similar to a mental state of being. It is in the mental realm that the Invisible Cause becomes visible, feelings turn into thoughts, ideas become prototypes, and desires motivate actions and reactions.

When Invisible Cause or Supreme Being thinks about or upon itself, it literally creates form and function, giving each a creative reason for life. In the universe, every form or phenomenon has cause for existence.

Science studies form and phenomenon to find the cause and or reason for behavior. For example, science looks at the effect of the Moon's gravity upon the Earth and concludes, in part, that the Moon is cause to tidal movements. This study is so effective that science can predict and measure the tides on any given day, all around the Earth.

## VISIBLE EFFECT

What happens in life, both mentally and physically, is called visible effect, or result, consequence, outcome, conclusion, fulfillment, beginning, end, purpose, significance, aftermath, accomplishment, etc. The most important distinction of visible effects is that they are temporary.

All effects are subject to change and were never intended for or capable of an infinite existence. As such, all who seek meaning in the world of effect are destined to remain confused and afraid because effects are fleeting.

The Body is the effect.
The Mind is the stage.
The Spirit is the actor.
The Play is Life Itself.

How does this all work in the Spirit, Mind, and Body of each individual person?

## SOUL AND SPIRIT

Spirit and Soul are popular words used by many to explain, illustrate, and define the nature of life and how it works. In The Science of Mind textbook, Soul is defined as the medium, agency, means, instrument, or atmosphere through which the Spirit of life passes into expression. The Soul is the sacred soil, the hallowed womb, and the fertile imagination ready to respond to Spirit's slightest desire, intention, or seed—thought.

Spirit thinks/selects, Soul creates/manifests. All life imitates this fundamental truth. From seeds to ideas, life is in a constant state of creation. A perpetual motion of invisible Cause moves through the Mind of humanity manifesting/ creating the visible effect of the world.

What Mozart hummed in his mind is still being played in the world. The love a mother gave to her child is still being given today. What someone was angry about yesterday, he or she may still be angry about today. This perpetual motion of seed thoughts, planted in the soil of humanity's mind, has the ability to recreate the effect of itself over and over. Repeatedly, our memory will play the same melody, give the same affection, and feel the same anger if we do not change our minds.

## How does one change humanity's mind?

Change your mind; change your life.

## Could it be that easy?

Yes, but keeping your mind changed is the challenge. In the mind of all humanity there exists the single most powerful force ever identified with the mental and physical experience of life: the memory.

What you think about all day long infuses your memory and repeatedly returns as your experience until you change your mind and keep it changed. To do this, you must learn to think in a productive, peaceful, and purpose-filled manner. You must find ways to work in concert with your Soul,

Spirit, Memory, the Powers of the Intuition, and the Tools of the Intellect.

## SUBJECTIVE SOUL

There is only one Soul, Mind, Spirit, and Body, but there are many individual experiences, mentalities, thoughts, and outcomes. Each human being is some part of God's mentality using Spirit and Soul to consciously or subconsciously create the visible effect of life.

The Soul is the creative and subjective servant of the Spirit that in psychology is sometimes called the subconscious—a sort of hidden agenda that is cause to your experience. Within the subjective parts of your human mentality, your piece of Soul, exists your memory and intuition.

Your memory is individual and collective, consisting of your own repetitive thoughts and the repetitive reactions of all humanity. In the absence of a consciously-directed, spiritually minded person, the memory will repeat all the old painful, boring, and limited patterns of the past. However, in the presence of a consciously directed, powerful conviction, old thoughts and limited beliefs can be erased and converted into a new and powerful mentality.

Such a positive mentality happens as the result of an expanded use of the powers of intention—namely life, love, light (understanding), beauty, peace, joy, and truth. All these powers flow from Invisible Cause, creating a Universal Soul Mentality that represents the infinite potential of the human race.

When used in prayer, these powers become the creative feelings and ideas of the Invisible Universal Intelligence of life, finding expression through a human mentality. As Ralph Waldo Emerson said, our lives and mentalities are a doorway through which God becomes personal.

## OBJECTIVE SPIRIT

The Soul must have the selective power of Spirit in order to express its creative potential. Spirit is inseparable from Soul and works by means of its intuitive and intellectual tools. Spirit is aware, selective, and objective (conscious) in its intent and desire.

In its intuitive mode, Spirit uses the powers of the Soul's intuition to gain access to the unlimited knowledge and potential of all life. In its highest form, Spirit uses its intellectual powers to center the Soul's attention on creating a healthy, prosperous, and happy life. In its most limited form, Spirit is forced to use its intellectual powers to compel the Soul's attention to the possibility of a disease-ridden, lonely, and poverty-stricken life. Either type of life is possible depending on what you choose to think about all day long.

Prayer is thought creating life according to the convictions of your beliefs. Prayer, like thought, is unceasing. Hence, in the absence of conscious prayer/ thought, mentality is directed by humanity's memory of failure and diseases, using the tools of your intellect to protect instead of grow, limit instead of expanding, and defend instead of love. In all cases, fear is the ultimate outcome.

**How does one heal humanity's catastrophic**

**memory?**

Use the ideas of Cause and Effect to explain the truth. Then, use your ability to align your mentality with God's Invisible Cause through Affirmative Prayer or Spiritual Mind Treatment.

Never allow your thoughts to be directed by humanity's memorized expectations of failure, rejection, disappointment, unhappiness, loneliness, poverty, or disease. Instead, train your mind to use its intellectual tools to perpetually predict a life of success.

Control your life by using the power of loving acceptance. Become motivated by using beauty, truth, peace, and joy as the criteria for all you weigh, measure, analyze, or compare when making decisions.

For instance, can you tell how much beauty, truth, peace, and joy is expressed in your words, thoughts, and deeds? Label every experience with the light of God's understanding and build a mentality of faith, acceptance, and belief.

# CHAPTER 11

# CREATING THE MENTALITY OF YOUR DESIRE

*Invisible Cause flows into expression according to your mentality. If you want a greater life, you must think greater and more affirmative thoughts.*

*Follow the suggested ideas and seek to create a mental picture of the feelings and qualities that reflect your highest ideals of living. Surrender only to the attitude of expectancy.*

*You are not the power; you are the mentality of God's power. Align yourself with the Divine and stay in the light of love. Your greatest good awaits your recognition!*

# TO CREATE THE MENTALITY OF YOUR DESIRE:

I.   Bring yourself back to Invisible Cause.

II.  Mentally see and feel yourself one with Cause.

III. Declare your result as if it were already done.

IV.  Accept and be thankful for all that is demonstrated.

V.   Release your word and let Divine Intelligence grow your life.

## I. Bring yourself back to Cause or Spirit.

- Cause creates life out of itself by some act upon itself through self-contemplation.

- Everything is created by Spirit and is therefore filled with Spirit's Intelligence.

- **AFFIRM:** I am, in total, a part of Cause's Intelligence and Divine Presence.

- Complete this statement:

*The Cause of life is ...*

_____

_____

_____

## II. See yourself as the activity of Cause.

- Endowed with Cause's Intuitive Intelligence, I create my world by contemplating Cause's love, beauty, power, peace, truth, and joy.

- I see the operation of my world in perfect harmony with the mentality of Cause's presence.

- **AFFIRM:** My Soul is now one with Cause's enthusiasm for creating my world successfully, creatively, and peacefully!

- Complete this statement:
*I am one with ...*

_____

_____

_____

# III. See Cause's mentality creating your life.

- It is Cause's mentality that creates my presence, and my presence is receptive to Spirit's mentality.

- Spirit's mentality now operates in all my conditions, relationships, reactions, and feelings.

- **AFFIRM:** There is no power in tension or conflict. The power is in the relaxed mentality of Spirit's complete love.

- Complete this statement:

*Right now, I am ...*

_____

_____

_____

## IV: Be thankful for all of Cause's blessings.

- Accept everything with the attitude of purposeful thanksgiving.

- Measure your flow of time, talent, and treasure. Dedicate a percentage of the flow to nurture whatever feeds and strengthens your divine mentality.

- **AFFIRM:** I dedicate myself to feeling the infinite love and complete presence of Cause's mentality.

- Complete this statement:

*I accept ...*

_____

_____

_____

## V. Let Cause's powers grow your life.

- Release all anticipation and worldly opinions about what it takes to be alive. Be here and be now.

- Release your affirmative word into the self-creating presence of Spirit's love.

- **AFFIRM:** I know and act in complete accord with the authority, power, and joy of Spirit's mentality.

- Complete this statement:

*Released, my word is now ...*

_____

_____

_____

# THINK OF IT THIS WAY

*I recognize the invisible authority of God's love as a state of mind. The power and nature of Divine Mind is sacred.*

*I unify with God's invisible and eternal creative Cause. I see my life done unto me as I believe.*

*I give thanks for this holy moment and sacred opportunity to partake in the love of life and the spirit of unconditional acceptance. I am guided by love.*

*I heal any memory or tendency toward error. I celebrate and affirm God's Love as Cause to my world, the purpose of my life, and the joy of my being.*

www.ingramcontent.com/pod-product-compliance
Lightning Source LLC
Chambersburg PA
CBHW052136090426
42741CB00009B/2108